Illustrated

by

Tony Benford

Copyright

Note from the Author

Dear Reader,

Prayer is a conversation between you and God. Have you ever wondered if He's listening? Have you ever wanted Him to speak to you? Well guess what? God is a great listener and He will speak to you! We not only serve a God that hears prayer but we serve a God of answered prayers! He answers through His Word and the Holy Spirit. In good times and challenging situations, He answers!

With love and kindness,

Tony Benford

I PRAYED AT THE POOL AND YOU ANSWERED.

I PRAYED AT MY SCHOOL AND YOU ANSWERED.

I PRAYED IN MY CLASS AND YOU ANSWERED.

I
NEEDED YOU
FAST AND
YOU ANSWERED.

I PRAYED iN THE LiGHT AND YOU ANSWERED.

I PRAYED IN THE NIGHT AND YOU ANSWERED.

I PRAYED AT THE STORE AND YOU ANSWERED.

A LITTLE BIT MORE AND YOU ANSWERED.

I PRAY FOR MY FREEDOM AND YOU ANSWERED.

I PRAY I CAN LEAD THEM AND YOU ANSWERED.

I PRAYED FOR MY HEALTH AND YOU ANSWERED.

FOR WISDOM IN WEALTH AND YOU ANSWERED.

WHEN I'M LOST AND I'M HURT, YOU ANSWERED.

YOU LED ME TO CHURCH. YOU ANSWERED.

LORD, I CALLED, AGAIN AND AGAIN...

MY LORD
MY KING
MY GOD
MY FRIEND.

YOU ANSWERED. AMEN!

DEDICATED TO CHANCELLOR LEE BENFORD

"THE MANTLE IS FOR THE CHANCELLOR."

MEN

40

OUGHT

41

TO

42

ALWAYS

PRAY

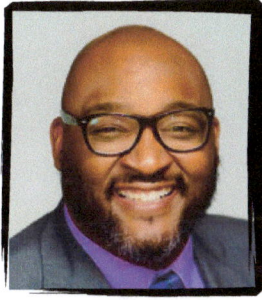

Have you ever wondered if God is really listening? Hello? is a powerful reminder that you don't need perfect words, a special line, or the right timing—because God is always on the main line, ready to hear your heart. With faith-filled encouragement and timely truth, Tony Benford invites you to tune in, speak up, and recognize that while God is always speaking, the real question is—are you listening? Let this book inspire you to answer His call and never miss the message meant just for you.

www.ingramcontent.com/pod-product-compliance
Lightning Source LLC
Chambersburg PA
CBHW041801040426

42447CB00005B/283